CW00552473

COLD WAR STEVE

THE ANNUAL 2024

CONSTABLE

**To Katy and Carl, without whom this book
would never have happened.**

CONSTABLE

First published in Great Britain in 2023 by Constable

13 5 7 9 10 8 6 4 2

Illustrations and captions © Christopher Spencer, 2023
Breaking America and Adequate Supplies © Carl Gosling, 2023
It Was Not a Party © James O'Brien, 2023
The Blood Tide © John Sweeney, 2023
The Emperor has No Clothes © Stewart Lee, 2023
The Vibes are Off! © Sheena Patel, 2023
The Egg and Spoon Race © Jason Williamson, 2023
Quiet Violence © Kit de Waal, 2023
Twenty-Four Hour Hearty People © Neville Southall and PJ Smith, 2023

The moral right of the author has been asserted.

All rights reserved.
p127 images: Duncan Raban/Popperfoto/Getty Images/Adobe Stock
No part of this publication may be reproduced, stored in a retrieval system,
or transmitted, in any form, or by any means, without the prior permission in
writing of the publisher, nor be otherwise circulated in any form of binding or
cover other than that in which it is published and without a similar condition
including this condition being imposed on the subsequent purchaser.

A CIP catalogue record for this book
is available from the British Library.

ISBN: 978-1-40871-977-0

Designed by Sian Rance at D. R. ink
Printed and bound in Italy by L.E.G.O. S.p.A.

Papers used by Constable are from well-managed forests
and other responsible sources.

Constable
An imprint of
Little, Brown Book Group
Carmelite House
50 Victoria Embankment
London EC4Y 0DZ

An Hachette UK Company
www.hachette.co.uk

www.littlebrown.co.uk

CONTENTS

THE COLD WAR STEVE ANNUAL has been an idea kicking around the office for as long as I can remember, filed next to the Cold War Steve fan club, convention and Christmas no 1. So, it is incredibly exciting to finally see this come to life, the inaugural edition you hold in your hands before you!

This book acts as a round-up of the year, or, in the case of this bumper first edition, features eighteen months of artwork from the mighty vaults of Christopher Spencer. It is a collection of his best work, his most cutting visual commentary, his most surreal, hilarious and tragic depictions of those in power and the state of the world.

Through humour, satire and a cast of ludicrous characters in dystopian settings, Cold War Steve's big, bold and often epic artworks attempt to explain how we ended up here, our national obsession with nostalgia, being ruled-over by hereditary weirdos and below-average political operators, and the absolute failure of our leaders to manage the country in this time of super-history and mega-crises – preferring instead to massage their mates' portfolios, or throw a giant free-for-all office party in the eye of the storm.

Cold War Steve shines a light through the thick fog of misinformation and political rhetoric on those who have brought out the worst in us all. But also, I think, he offers hope

INTRODUCTION

for the future through positive activism, common sense, collaboration and the good people out there who inspire us and actively push for greater common good within our communities every day.

It is a great honour and delight to have some exclusive contributions within these pages as well. Somehow we managed to gather an A-list cast of writers including James O'Brien on 'Partygate', award winning novelist Sheena Patel, Jason Williamson of Sleaford Mods, John Sweeney live from Ukraine, Kit de Waal invoking Jonathan Swift, comedian Stewart Lee, and former international goalkeeper Neville Southall in conversation with Liverpudlian spoken word hero PJ Smith, AKA Roy.

Good people, join us as we pull back the curtain.

IT WAS
NOT
A PARTY

JAMES O'BRIEN

IN THE BEGINNING, there were no parties. Of this Boris Johnson was absolutely certain. We know because he said so. In the House of Commons on 1 December 2021: 'What I can tell the right honourable and learned gentleman is that all guidance was followed completely in No 10.' And on the BBC on 7 December: 'All the guidelines were observed.'

The next day, alas, footage emerged of his press secretary, Allegra Stratton, joking with Downing Street colleagues about a 'Downing Street Christmas party on Friday night'. Johnson, who both lived and worked in Downing Street, was sickened and furious. We know because he said so: 'I apologise for the impression that has been given that staff in Downing Street take this less than seriously. I am sickened myself and furious about that, but I repeat what I have said . . . I have been repeatedly assured that the rules were not broken. I repeat that I have been repeatedly assured since these allegations emerged that there was no party and that no Covid rules were broken.'

He instructed Simon Case, the cabinet secretary and head of the civil service, to investigate the claims. After reports that Case had attended one of the parties, he was forced to remove himself from the investigation. He was replaced by experienced civil servant Sue Gray.

Within a week, the story would change again. While it was no longer the case that there hadn't been *any* parties, Boris Johnson was adamant that he knew nothing about them and certainly hadn't been anywhere near them. We know because he said so. On Sky News on 13 December: 'I can tell you once again that I certainly broke no rules . . . all that is being looked into.'

One week later, photographs emerged of Downing Street staff, including Boris Johnson, his then fiancé and their new baby, attending what looked a lot like a drinks party in the Downing Street garden. There were even cheese boards. It was not, however, a party. We know because he said so. On 20 December on the BBC: 'Those were people at work, talking about work. I have said what I have to say about that.'

Nevertheless, by 12 January he was apologising for attending the work event that was definitely not a party. In his garden. Attended by his wife and child. It was, in fact, a 'bring your own booze' work event. We know because he said so. To the House of Commons: 'I believed implicitly that this was a work event, but with hindsight, I should have sent everyone back inside.'

Anyway, there was certainly no party *inside* Downing Street on 13 November 2020. We know because he said so. In the House of Commons: 'No, but I am sure that whatever happened, the guidance was followed, and the rules were followed, at all times.'

Eighteen months later, four photographs emerged of him raising a glass to toast his director of communications, Lee Cain, at a party in Downing Street on 13 November 2020. Some attendees received police fines. Johnson did not.

He did, however, get one for attending his own birthday party. In Downing Street. On 19 June 2020. It was also attended by his then fiancé and her interior decorator. Johnson would insist it was a work gathering where he was 'ambushed by cake'.

By this point, most people had lost count of all the parties. Including the vomit-strewn affairs that unfolded on the eve of Prince Philip's funeral. Johnson loyalists continued to insist that there hadn't been any and that, even if there had, he couldn't possibly have been expected to know about them. Especially the ones he actually attended. In the building where he lived and worked.

In total, the Metropolitan Police would make 126 referrals for fixed penalty notices, to eighty-three people, with twenty-eight people receiving between two and five fines. All for parties that never, according to Boris Johnson, happened.

Sue Gray would find 'failures of leadership and judgement in No 10 and the Cabinet Office' for which 'the senior leadership at the centre, both political and official, must bear responsibility'. Johnson, who has never borne responsibility for anything in his life, survived a vote of no confidence but would stand down as PM a few weeks later after a mass resignation of his own ministers.

So, to be absolutely clear: there definitely weren't any parties and then there were parties but he definitely didn't attend them, and then there were parties and he did attend them but he definitely didn't realise they were parties, and then there were parties and he did attend them and got a police fine for doing so. And the Sue Gray report was simultaneously a damp squib and a witch-hunt. But he still got all the big calls right. ●

Just when you thought that Dominic Cummings and his Barnard Castle 'testing his eyes' bollocks was surely the peak of utter contempt a government could display towards the British public — along came partygate!

We all know No 10 loves to throw a shit party: crap Christmas jumpers, sweaty cheeseboards and wine by the suitcase. Does it matter who actually attended the parties and who didn't? Does it fuck. They are all responsible.

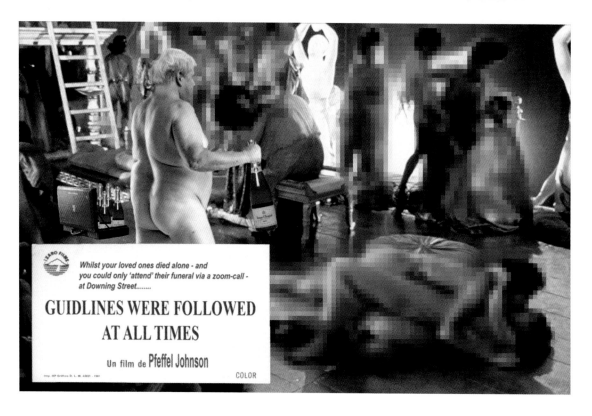

Whilst your loved ones died alone - and you could only 'attend' their funeral via a zoom-call - at Downing Street........

GUIDLINES WERE FOLLOWED AT ALL TIMES

Un film de **Pfeffel Johnson**

COLOR

THIS IS YOUR LI E

Partygate ought to have triggered mass riots and civil unrest. However, in this land of *Daily Mail* readers, the most we could expect (and got) was the occasional roll of an apathetic eye and stifled tut.

The Sue Grey report — much like the Russia report from a few years ago — was devoid of any real accountability. Johnson's jumbo redacting marker (and 'forgotten' mobile phone passwords) probably ensured as much.

Whilst more and more tawdry details of partygate came to light, my indignation intensified. As I've always done, I channelled my anger into my art. In using backdrops of, say, the Covid Memorial Wall, I reflect on whether I've gone 'too far' or been 'too crass and disrespectful'? Well, no, frankly. However distasteful my collage may initially seem, it barely touches the sides of how distasteful these bastards have been.

THE BLOOD TIDE JOHN SWEENEY

SAY WHAT YOU LIKE about Vladimir Putin – he's a serial killer, after all – but it's fair to say that he is the most successful fascist ruler since Adolf Hitler. Like Hitler, he could only get away with his mass murders because of the complacency, fear and greed of Western leaders. George W. Bush, Tony Blair, Barack Obama, Gordon Brown, David Cameron, Donald Trump, Theresa May, Boris Johnson, Rishi Sunak and the lettuce woman all let Putin get away with murder, time and time again.

Putin likes killing. The blood tide started in September 1999 with the Moscow apartment bombs. The master of the Kremlin blamed these on Chechen terrorists, but the evidence is overwhelming that the bomb outrages, which killed more than three hundred Russians, were, in fact, a black operation by the FSB – new name for the KGB. Old dog, same tricks. The apartment bombs were used as an excuse to start the Second Chechen War. No one knows how many people in this pitiless war because no one counted but one estimate is sixty thousand dead. In 2000, I went undercover to Chechnya twice and first called Putin a war criminal twenty-three years ago in the pages of my old paper, the *Observer*. No one listened because I was outvoted by a ton of Moscow gold flowing through the sewers of the city of London.

Reading correctly just how pitifully corrupt and corruptible Londongrad was, Putin carried on killing. Half of London was littered with polonium-210 when his goons poisoned former KGB spy Alexander Litvinenko. Britain reacted by expelling four Russian spies. Putin hit print on his diplomatic passport machine four times and moved on, poisoning or otherwise killing his domestic and external opposition.

Poisoned then shot, shot, shot: that's what happened to Anna Politkovskaya, Natalya Estemirova and Boris Nemtsov. Putin played footsie with the West through his proxy-oligarchs. The deal is they can keep their dirty money so long as they owe fealty to him. Roman Abramovich snapped up Chelsea, Oleg Deripaska wooed first Peter Mandelson, then George Osborne. As Russian gold became dirtier by the hour, largesse with snow on its boots was dolloped out by the outer oligarchs, especially to members of the Conservative Party. Please note there is no such thing as an anti-Kremlin Russian oligarch.

Putin first moved into Ukraine in 2014, gobbling up Crimea and half of the eastern oblasts or counties of Donetsk and Luhansk. Then a Russian BUK missile shot MH17 out of the sky, killing all 298 people on board, including ten Britons. Once again, the British government did nothing serious to signal our displeasure to the Kremlin, so he carried on with the murdering. Salisbury got poisoned in 2018 by novichok. Britain retaliated by expelling spies so that all Putin had to do was hit print on his diplomatic passport machine, again. (Putin's hots for poison, I suspect, comes from his Leningrad upbringing. His block of flats was infested with rats. Poison was the best method of fighting the enemy, then and now, the more exotic the better.)

Back in 2018, Boris Johnson, then the foreign secretary, left a critical NATO meeting in Brussels which had determined the slapped wrist for Putin and went straight to a bunga bunga party thrown by former KGB spy Alexander Lebedev in his *palazzo* in Italy. Boris partied without his British police protection team, meaning that there was no one to keep an eye on what he got up to under a Russian roof. Down the track, Boris made Lebedev's

stupid boy, Evgeny, Baron Siberia. There is, of course, no suggestion that the KGB committed any wrongdoing. True, Johnson moved fast to help Ukraine when Russia declared its big war in February 2022, but that was far too little, far too late. The damage had been done.

Ukraine's extraordinary courage and resilience has spelt out a couple of things our rulers have forgotten: that democracy must be defended and that free speech does not come free. Putin's poison high tide, it seems, came in 2016 when two Kremlin wet dreams came true: first Brexit, then Trump. People in Britain are waking up to the Brexit omnishambles, but the majority of the Republican party are still loyal to a leader who fawns before Putin. Hitler was never that successful.

How has Vladimir Putin got away with killing so many people for so long? I met him once in 2014 when, working for BBC Panorama, I pretended to be a professor of mammothology and rocked up at some old bones museum in Siberia, hijacking the proceedings by challenging Putin about the shooting down of MH17. Putin lied through his teeth. Later, a silent goon punched me in the stomach. I guess they didn't like my question. But what was striking is that Putin did not come across all masterful to me. On the contrary, he was surprisingly effeminate, almost submissive. Mick Herron, the author of the brilliant *Slough House* spy novels, has his fictional MI5 boss call Putin 'the Gay Hussar'. Putin is, I suspect, a psychopath in denial of his sexuality, someone who grew up in dire poverty, who became, through cunning, adept at exploiting the weaknesses of others. Mystery sticks to who his real mother and father were but one psychiatrist believes that, like Hitler, Mao and Stalin, he was rejected or abandoned by his natural mother very early on.

Long before he became a spy, he was a gangster. The pimp-roll as he struts into the Kremlin's great hall, the love of gangster-speak, the carnal ecstasy he derives from watching his under-bosses fight to establish their loyalty, that's the mafia at work and at play. What is so grimly fascinating is that his apprenticeship in the grime of Leningrad worked, too, with the likes of Bush and Blair, Trump and Johnson. Like Hitler, Putin has got away with so much because he is a psychopath standing on the shoulders of pygmies. ●

As with the Covid pandemic, I was unsure if I should really be creating satirical collages about such a harrowing world event. I decided to initially focus my cosmic cynicism upon the hypocrisy of Tory ministers who were suddenly taking the moral high ground over Putin when they'd been snaffling up his (and his oligarchs') grubby roubles for years.

I mean, how are we supposed to take these fuckers seriously? In these grave times of war in Europe and millions of families in Britain living in abject poverty, we have the most inept, duplicitous, woefully inadequate government in British history.

Kyiv, il 16 giugno 2022

16 червня 2022 року
Київ

Le 16 juin 2022, à Kyiv

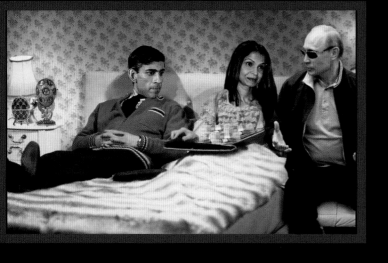

Oligarchs and donors first.

THE EMPEROR HAS NO CLOTHES

STEWART LEE

A CONSERVATIVELY MINDED critic snorting over their *Spectator* might consider Cold War Steve's work, its anger and disgust, so near the surface, unsubtle and bombastic; a chaotic punk and Pritt Stick alternative to the dry satirical nuances of *The Thick of It* or *Veep*, for example. Armando Iannucci's tasteful TV satires share Cold War Steve's disillusion with due political process, but do not deploy the heavy artillery of images of a naked Prime Minister trussed up like a suckling pig.

But how can any response be too extreme for the times we live in, and the personalities that inhabit them? This is, after all, the era of Boris Piccaninny Watermelon Letterbox Cake Bumboys Vampires Haircut Wall-Spaffer Spunk-Burster Fuck-Business Fuck-The-Families Get-Off-My-Fucking-Laptop Girly-Swot Big-Girl's-Blouse Chicken-Frit Hulk-Smash Noseringed-Crusties Death-Humbug Technology-Lessons Surrender-Bullshit French-Turds Dog-Whistle Get-Stuffed FactcheckUK@CCHQ 88 Per Cent-Lies Get-Brexit-Done Bung-A-Bob-For-Big-Ben's-Bongs Cocaine-Event Spiritual-Worth Three-Men-and-a-Dog Whatever-It-Takes I-Shook-Hands-With-Everyone Herd-Immunity I-Want-To-Thank-Po-Ling Squash-The-Sombrero Parliamentary-Witch-Hunt I-Forgot-My-Pin-Number Johnson.

In regard to Boris Johnson, rational critique and sensible satire are swotted away; inconvenient facts about misdemeanors are dismissed as 'inverted piles of piffle', incriminating mobile phones are mislaid, uncomfortable questions are avoided by walking into a walk-in fridge, justice is evaded. Again. And again. And again. Boris Johnson's former ally, the blancmange-faced Peasemore fistula David Cameron, described his Etonian schoolmate as avoiding capture like a 'greased piglet'.

But even the greasiest piglet does not escape the ire of Cold War Steve's collages, and they grow ever more ambitious, like sumptuous Renaissance paintings of a corrupt court, peopled with the personalities that flourished in Boris Johnson's sewage-filled wake; inexplicably inflated non-entities waving explanatory placards, like James Gilroy caricatures in clipped pin-sharp shapes; the KGB agent's ennobled son, omnipresent and unaccountable; that violinist; two dutiful wives (one blurred), the publicly funded pole dancer and that mysterious youthful life peer, all in the same portentous railway scene; that violinist; dozens of distracting Schofields, televised, with bodies buried behind them; that violinist; the vomiting and puking ministers departing party central as cleaners on minimum wage move in masks to mop up their mess; that violinist; the delusional culture secretary in her attic shrine; that violinist; that violinist; that violinist.

One day, if rational analysis survives the rise of fake news and opaquely funded Tufton St disinformation, Boris Johnson will be acknowledged as a liar and cheat, a narcissist who discredited democracy and perhaps irrevocably degraded British politics, and a man who took us, disastrously, out of the European Union on false pretenses simply to further his own career. And then our culturally and financially impoverished children will ask us, what we did to stop him? The answer is not enough. Some of us didn't even vote, let alone take to the streets. Instead, we said, 'It's Boris innit?'

But Cold War Steve's conscience is clear. Look. He has shown Boris Johnson hanging naked and fat-arsed from a Downing Street window; and Boris Johnson naked flinging dung in parliament; and Boris Johnson in tiny pants taking a sledgehammer to the office of Prime Minister and then fleeing with it on fire; and Boris Johnson naked trailing Rule Britannia bunting from his anus; and Boris Johnson, naked and laughing, driving a *Daily Mail* muck-spreader past a mass grave. The Emperor has no clothes. It's not up for debate! No one could have done more. Greater love hath no man than Cold War Steve. ●

It came as absolutely no surprise to anyone (well, anyone who hadn't been radicalised by the right-wing press), that the premiership of Alexander Boris de Pfeffel Johnson would end in this way. A proven pathological liar whose actions are only ever determined by what's in his best interest, not the best interest of the country. He destroys everything and everyone he comes into contact with . . . but, with a bit of mumbled Latin (and quick 'messing up' of his hair), the radicalised masses forgive him and he moves on to the next self-indulgent fuck-up with complete impunity.

De Pfeffel's leaving speech: a bloviating, narcissistic sack of baboon shit to the end. No contrition or self-awareness. He truly believes that rules do not apply to him.

The vibes are off she kept saying very loudly to anyone who could hear her, but no one laughed even though she thought it was a very funny joke. A friend over the phone told her he was talking to a colleague and the colleague said everyone is miserable, and she said, yes, the vibes are off! She kept trying to make the joke happen but no one else wanted to laugh. She would keep trying.

THE VIBES ARE OFF!

The lettuce reached a sort of manic hysteria. It was in response to a joke made in an article that then another paper took literally, set up a lettuce with a video cam and live streamed it and then asked the internet, which would last longer: the lettuce or the Prime Minister? She was recalling this from memory. The idea of googling the exact words filled her with some dread and anyway no one listened to facts, she thought, this, staying faithful to what actually historically happened, was not in tune with the people.

The boy queen had his allowance increased from 80 odd million to 125 odd million when hundreds of thousands of ordinary people had been striking, could barely afford to pay for food, small business owners were going under, children turned up to school or didn't, and this was all really normal. Everything was normal.

No one was allowed to say the 'B' word and no, I don't mean the name of the previous Prime Minister – not the lettuce one who said a few words somewhere and then everyone's mortgages went bananas (keep up) which only meant that they felt the same pain as renters, and not the name of the one who partied and then lied about it and then was allowed to get away with the lie and then bought a house worth millions in Oxford and had made five million since leaving office, at the last count. Who was the real loser, eh? It was the *other* 'B' word we were not allowed to talk about, the old 'B' word, the one from such hits as, the 'Sunlit Uplands'. We were in a collective system reset and we couldn't talk about it. Our problems have come out from thin air – or Putin or Ukraine or small boats or ULEZ. Anything to win a few hundred votes. No one would say the 'B' word wasn't working. However, the EU and America had moved on, there were conferences and talks which we were not invited to anymore and it was fine. We didn't want to be there anyway.

The Queue, that's what it had been shortened to. No, not the one to see a doctor. Someone secured a book deal using The Queue as a backdrop. They said it would be a romance.

There was a point where doctors stopped asking patients who the Prime Minister was because it was too confusing. That was, if you could even see a doctor. The queue to see one was very long but it was part of the character of the people, to wait in a queue.

Her dad joined The Queue and he had voted for the 'B' word, no, not *that* 'B' word, not the one who partied. She couldn't bear to look at her dear old dad when he came back. Her mother said, I would have gone if my leg was better. She'd been waiting three months for an appointment to see the doctor at the hospital, couldn't get an appointment to see the GP unless she threatened the receptionist with violence and hardened her tone. Her parents, the staunch monarchists – but then the system had worked for them. Hadn't it? It was all working as it was supposed to be working. Everything was completely normal.

The Prime Minister, no, not the one who partied and then lied about it and was then allowed to get away with the lie and then bought a house worth millions in Oxford and has made five million since leaving office, and not the one with the lettuce, I mean the one who seemed to disappear, the one who, unsurprisingly, was the most racist of all. He had decided that migrant barges full of Brown people were a fantastic idea and were what ordinary people wanted, even though holidaying Britons were fleeing wild fires in Greece in small boats and were greeted with a different kind of hospitality and not the kind of hospitality which met the Ukrainian refugees which started well but is now going badly. No one could mention the differing treatment of people based on the colour of their skin because that was frankly racist.

A user on the newly reformed 'X' website said that the country was being run by people who would have got kicked out in the first week of *The Apprentice*. We now talked of events in the country as if they were a season on a television drama because why not? Weren't we mere spectators to history?

She could really do with no more historical events. Too much history had happened. But she thought it was important to witness the sinking of a country. To really be here. Absorb it. ●

SHEENA PATEL

The queue to see the Queen's coffin stretched for miles. Patriotic queuers were provided with blankets, water and warm sustenance to help maintain their plucky steadfastness. The line of loyal lamenters wound its way past many London landmarks such as the HMS Belfast, Tate Modern, London Eye . . . and, of course, hundreds of freezing, hungry homeless people.

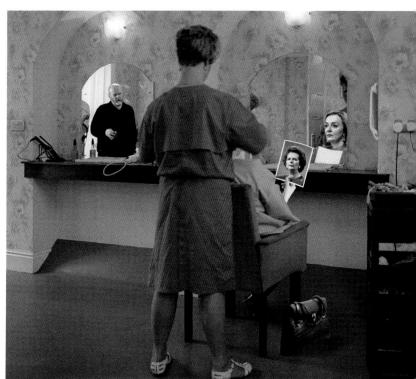

FOOD
BANK

1952 E II R 2022

Shoe Zone

The Truss tenure. Forty-five days as Prime Minister. She had promised to reinvigorate the British economy and put it on the path to long-term success. Her *Stars in Their Eyes* incarnation as the new Margaret Thatcher was in full flow. The Truss/Kwarteng (AKA Tufton Street) mini budget, announced just three weeks after she had taken office, was cheered by all the usual right-wing commentators . . . It was a disaster, which resulted in driving the pound to record lows, sparking chaos on bond markets and increasing mortgage costs for millions of people. Truss fired Kwasi Kwarteng, but it was not enough to prevent her becoming the shortest serving Prime Minister in British history.

THE EGG AND
SPOON RACE

CHARLES'S CORONATION. The egg and spoon race of all egg and spoon races. It was funny as fuck, watching Camilla balance the big furry tower of jewels on her head as she tried to walk over to Charles's side. These days the royal stash looks homemade, like odd bits of shiny tat you keep telling your kids to throw out; papier-mâché, oversized daft shit. As she wobbled over after being crowned, you could see Charles trying not to laugh. It was insane.

Except for Andrew, it seems, gone is the utter disdain for these folks, the cut and paste hatred for the Windsors is not, in the minds of those that are more reasoned, a thing anymore. We've given up demanding that they turn in their guns and badges because we have so many newer problems caused by slightly less loaded bastards in important jobs putting daft ideas into the hordes of public that these cunts influence. I mean, I say cunts, but are they? Are the Windsors cunts? I imagine they can be agreeable people in interpersonal conversation. It's a shit tip on one side and a shit tip on the other. Restaurants with helicopter landing pads obscured by miles of woodland are not going to give you complete peace of mind. Luxury can only hold a small part of your escape from life, surely?

Given the amount of damage the government has done since it limped to power in 2011 or whenever, the £50 to £100 million spent on the Coronation wouldn't get you a Happy Meal. It wouldn't do much, would it, in relation to the tortured cerebrum of this, the public's psychology. We are at the rotten core now, with nothing but the brown bits to press our nose against as the giant pips stab and penetrate our flesh. We are the open bank for those who can take from it. The inflamed joints of collective frustration whose only access to the world beyond our own is through reality TV shows concerning those that have the financial bedding to levy onto themselves a life fantastic.

But then, why do they all uphold such damning scaffolding for millions of people to suffer under? You think about the cost of Charles's Coronation and all that papier-mâché. Between £50 to £100 million paid for by us. Why us? The primal response is, well it's because they are fucking bastard branches belonging to a big bastard tree that doesn't give a fuck about us or our

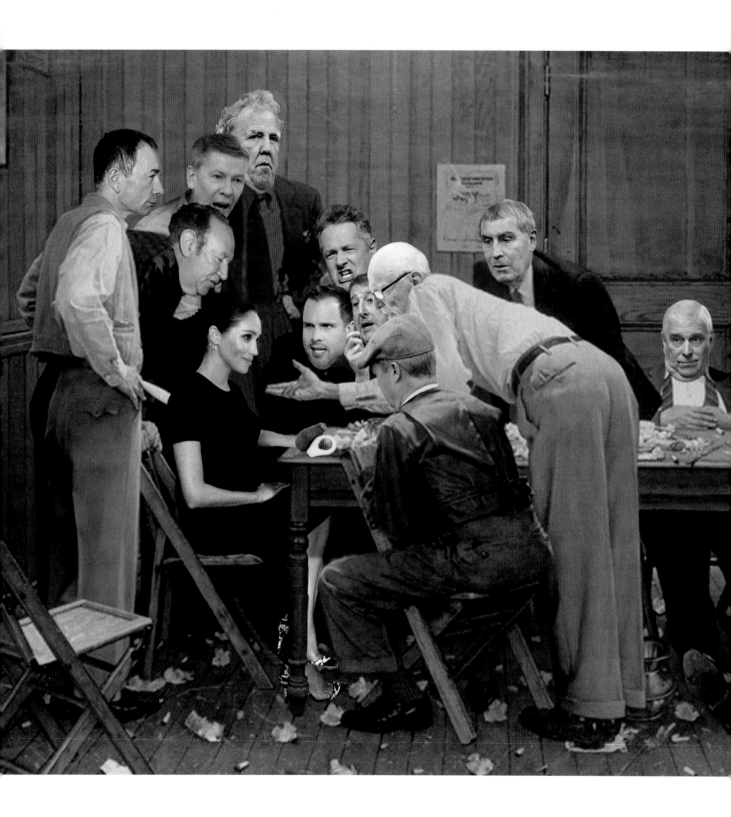

'A young healthy baby well nursed is, at a year old, a most delicious nourishing and wholesome food whether stewed, roasted, baked or boiled and I make no doubt that it will equally serve in a fricassee or a ragout'

Jonathon Swift, *A Modest Proposal*, 1729

JONATHON SWIFT'S SATIRICAL suggestion was made in response to the dire conditions faced by Irish people in the early eighteenth century due to British political oppression and exploitation. Like the rest of the empire, Ireland was used primarily as a source of raw material with most of its valuable resources shipped to England, notably wheat and grain but also wool, livestock, timber, fish and labour. This, along with high taxes, no independent parliament and some of the most savage penal laws in the empire, caused widespread famine, disease, poverty and homelessness and, worst of all, disempowerment and cultural suppression.

Charles Trevelyan, the English MP in charge of famine relief at the time, thought that the consequential death from not having enough to eat could be seen, usefully, as a mechanism for reducing the surplus population in Ireland and that, rather than intervene with aid, England should allow the market to level itself naturally. Other politicians at the time, called the Irish 'white savages' and dismissed their plight as being the fault of a lack of self-discipline and hard work.

QUIET VIOLENCE

Attitudes towards the poor haven't changed much in nearly three hundred years. In 2020, Lee Anderson, MP for Ashfield, said 'I know in my heart of hearts that this government will leave no stone unturned to help those most in need and if that means children going hungry, as we saw this summer, then so be it.' He later doubled-down on his attitude to the poor saying that people could live quite easily on meals made for 30p, harking back to Iain Duncan Smith's assertions in 2013 that he could live on the modern equivalent of £7.57 per day. Clearly, they both have a better grasp of budgeting than the feckless wasters that have to do it day in day out.

Similarly, Jacob Rees-Mogg in 2018 declared the rise in foodbanks 'uplifting' and said the increase in their use was driven by 'supply not demand'. In other words, there are not really 2.99 million people in food poverty queuing up for a couple of carry bags of basic meals because they have no choice. On the contrary, there are millions of people with surplus food that simply need somewhere to put it and greedy opportunists taking without real need.

The similarities between British politics and policies today and at Swift's time don't stop with poverty. In 2022, new legislation granted the government powers to curtail our right to protest and for vulnerable people to seek asylum. The cost-of-living crisis continues to disproportionately affect those who already struggle with everyday essentials like energy and food, with outgoings rising much faster than household income, on top of unaffordable rent and mortgages.

You could buckle under the weight of bad news. You could turn off the telly and disengage from the endless stream of negativity and fear. Or, you could get your digital scissors out and make a collage.

Like Swift, Cold War Steve's humour is bleak and biting. By placing politicians and commentators in absurd situations and costumes, he's drawing attention to what they are really saying and how dangerously close they come to aligning themselves with some of the darkest periods of human history. Complex, intricate, clever and challenging, his work highlights the disconnect between those in power and ordinary people, between what politicians say and what they really mean, between where we think we are and where we are going.

I have no idea if Cold War Steve's work changes minds and hearts. Maybe it does but that's not the intention. For many of us, his collages are a coping mechanism for our frustrations and despair. We peer in close – you have to – and find tiny details you missed on first look; you zoom out and it could almost be an old master or a child's cartoon. This is powerful stuff. The picture of a single Black woman surrounded by a dozen, braying, middle aged white men is horrific in its quiet violence. An ecstatic Suella Braverman at the helm of a rescue boat being rowed through a sea of drowning refugees is gut-churning.

These pictures speak to the truth of what we feel without speaking at all and call for an awakening and a reckoning. And, despite everything, they are a message of hope and resilience, needed now more than ever. ●

KIT DE WAAL

What have we become? How have hate, ignorance and a complete lack of compassion become the desired characteristics – and policies – of our government? While anyone opposed to such regressive attitudes are dismissed as being woke 'libtards' (or some other similarly inane portmanteau). Using 'woke' (i.e. being alert to prejudice and discrimination) as a pejorative is where we are now. And it's fucked up. And heartbreaking.

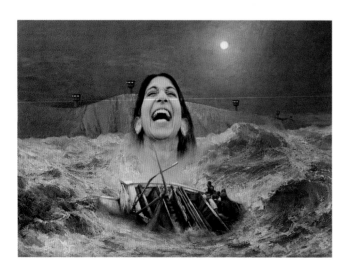

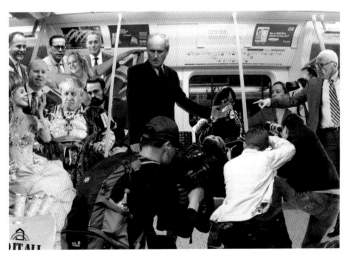

It is clear that the Tories' main tactic for fighting the next General Election will be the 'culture wars'. Wheel out a useful idiot like 30p Lee Anderson to spout fascistic bollocks and demean the poor. Divert people's attention from your own corruption and depravity by referring to asylum seekers as 'an invasion' whilst shouting, 'stop the boats!' Manipulate voters (who are unable to afford to heat their homes) into believing 'lefty lawyers' are the greatest threat to their lives.

ONE MIGHT THINK that Cold War Steve is a quintessentially British affair with the fringe of UK celebrities; a cast of uniquely inadequate politicians from Westminster; dilapidated high streets; the faded grandeur of the seaside and warm timeless glow of our working men's clubs; and, perhaps, a particular British brand of humour too. But all this hasn't stopped Chris's work being seen across the Atlantic. Back in 2019 when Brexit was still the biggest story on UK shores, Cold War Steve was commissioned by *Time* magazine to illustrate the madness into which we had by then descended. That was swiftly followed by a stateside CWS Office recce to Las Vegas (Chris pictured here with the Republican Party's presidential candidate, 2028), a trip to the world's greatest Evel Knievel-themed pizza restaurant and Red Rock to eat some canyon. Cold War Steve wanted to break the USA!

BREAKING AMERICA

Of course, America has its own galactic-scale wallies, conspiracy nuts, bozo billionaires, political chaos and societal and ecological collapse to contend with, which has often featured in Chris's work. It is no laughing matter though – the rise and rise again of Trump is a collective madness created by a complex set of circumstances in America and the world at large. Anger with established political class, capitalism's increasing sickness, a global growth obsession based on cheap labour and technology destroying our minds and freewill. The US is staring once again into an orange abyss. Women's reproductive rights are in question, a sexual predator and climate changer denier is heading for the White House and America burns whilst the world's richest man heads for the moon.

Cold War Steve needs to break America before it breaks itself. ●

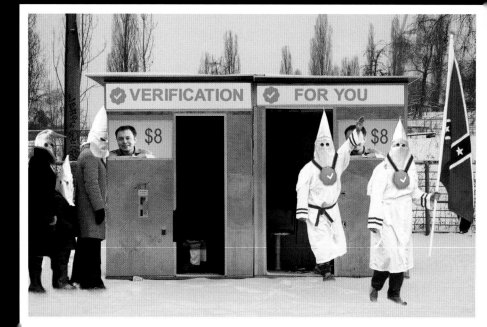

Twitter was always a bit of toxic bear pit —
but with some judicious muting and self-
control (not to respond or react to trolls)
it was OK. I mean, it's where I 'made it'
after all. However, since it has been taken
over by the petulant, attention-seeking
manbaby, it has become an unbearable
cesspool of fascists.

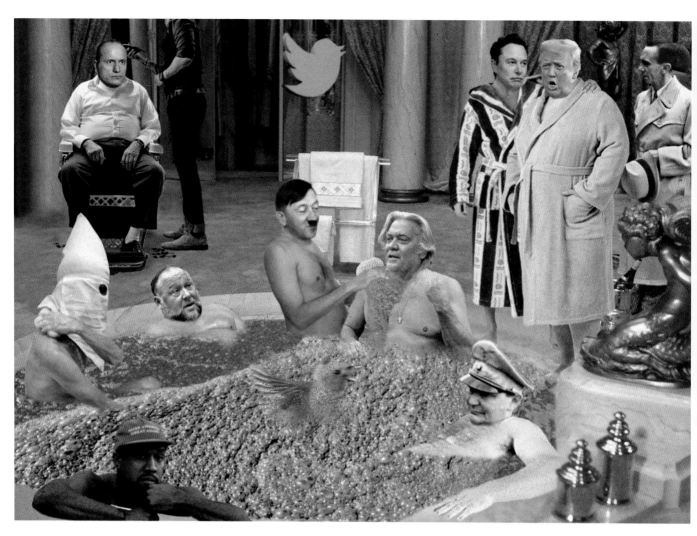

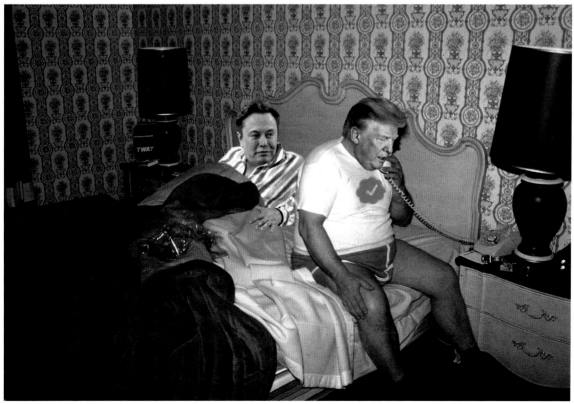

The return of Trump. More deranged, more unhinged, more delusional than ever. He has recently been indicted on a total of ninety-one federal and state charges for an array of crimes including 'risking national security secrets' and trying to 'subvert democracy'. His demented acolytes are sticking with him, even chipping in to pay for the Billionaire's legal fees.

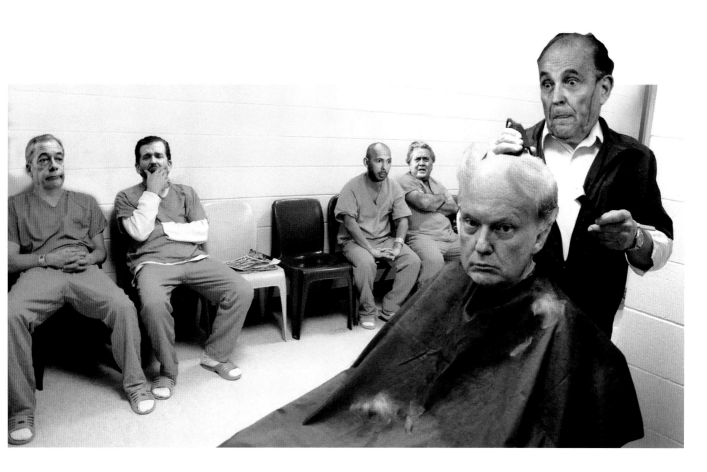

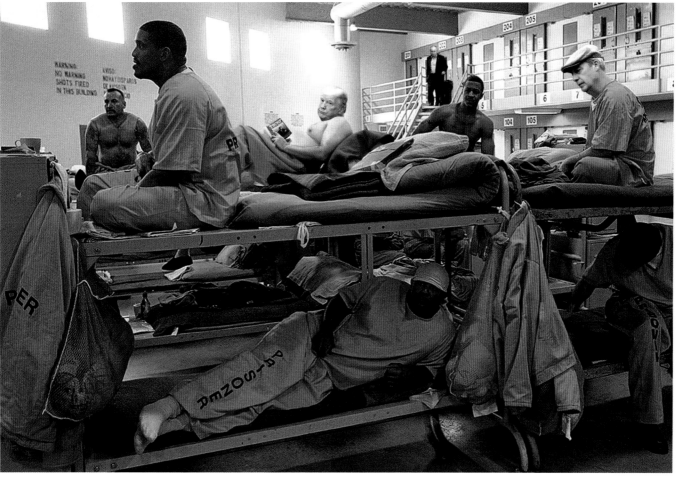

Cold war Steve after WM. BALFOUR-KER.

STRIKE TO SAVE THE NHS
Kick out the Tories

HEALTH WORKERS NEED A PAY RISE. SAVE OUR NHS! BUILD FOR A 24HR GENERAL STRIKE
socialistparty.org.uk

SUPPORT YOUR POSTIE NOT CORPORATE GREED !!

CUT PROFITS NOT JOBS & SERVICES
RMT
SUPPO ANSPOR

CLAPS DON'T PAY THE BILLS

DON'T MAKE PENSIONERS CHOOSE BETWEEN HEATING OR EATING

SAVE OUR ROYAL MAIL
CWU
#StandByYourPost

FAIR PAY FOR NURSING
It's time to pay nursing staff fairly

DEFEN Rail

PAY CONDIT

N THE VOI NU

WE WERE PROMISED adequate food by Dominic Raab (top Tory bully and former Brexit Secretary) in the case of a no-deal Brexit back in 2018. I guess this was supposed to calm any nerves we had about the cliff edge ahead, but what big Dom didn't realise then was that there would barely be any shops left at all by 2034.

High streets across the nation entirely shuttered from Telford to Torbay after a torturous and gradual deterioration. Landlords abandoned looking for any new tenants or pop-up shops and instead sat on their idle property wealth and imagined better times ahead. All the while impoverished local councils ran community art competitions to try and brighten up the sea of boarded up B&Ms.

ADEQUATE SUPPLIES

One household name after another fell – what started with Dixons and Debenhams, Woolworths and Wilkos, saw giants like Boots, JD Sports and M&S eventually follow. Even the bubble tea, vape and pound shops succumbed after TikTok's acquisition of Amazon.

The last chain standing, of course, was Adequate Supplies: Cold War Steve's historic family business which finally relaunched in the summer of 2024 after years of speculation. Backed by a mysterious Gulf-based sovereign wealth fund, the store stepped in to fill the void left by Greggs, selling its White Dog Shit ™ range of collectables. The second iteration of the chain prospered for a short time, making Christopher Spencer a millionaire and becoming one of our most unlikely and sadly final high street success stories. ●

COLD WAR STEVE OFFICE

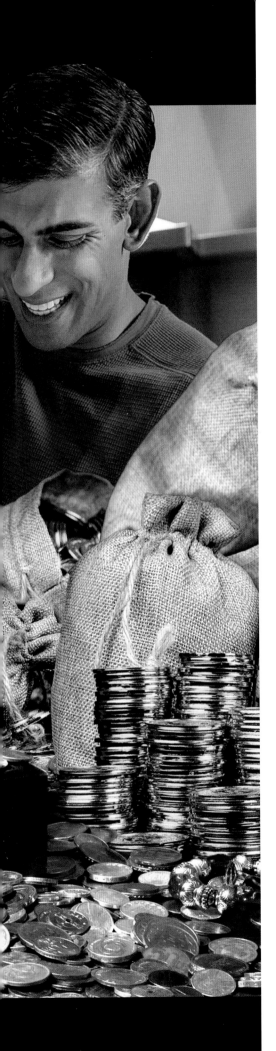

Roy: Let's get this out of the way first. This is nothing to do with football. I will say, though, that I am an Evertonian who was a kid during the 1980s. My favourite players were mostly all attackers: Gary Lineker, Graeme Sharp, Kevin Sheedy, Adrian Heath. People who scored goals. They were the ones whose names I shouted as I booted a ball against a wall in L4. In 1987, I shocked my mum by saying, 'Can I have the goalie kit this season please, Ma, with a number one on the back?' I think most Everton kids went through this stage at some point during the '80s. The reason for this is simple. Neville Southall. The greatest goalkeeper in the world. Keep reading – I promise you there's much more to this than football.

Fast forward thirty-odd years and here I am sat on my couch in the middle of a Zoom call with Neville himself. Nowadays, he is known as much more than a great goalkeeper. His family, friends and teammates have known this all along, of course. For most people though, it was Neville's Twitter account that alerted the rest of us. He has used it as a force for good: a platform to give under-represented groups and minorities a voice; an opportunity for him to learn more about the ever-changing world around him. Social media is a bit like drugs and those e-scooters. If you're able to use them properly, they can improve your life. Fuck about with them, though, and the thing will go very pear shaped, very quickly. You're now imagining Neville scootering down Goodison road, smoking a reefer, aren't you? If anyone can, Neville can. One handed, like he did with that Man United cross in the 1995 FA Cup final. That's it. No more football chat. I promise.

Neville, we spoke about what we wanted to contribute to this esteemed tome. Conversation quickly turned to how we keep ourselves mentally well in an era characterised by cruelty, dread and anxiety. You mentioned a simple concept that is very familiar to me. The practice of taking things one day at a time.

Neville: As a footballer you get your head down. You play Saturday or Sunday, then you worry about Tuesday. You play Tuesday, then you think about Saturday again. Before you know it, ten to fifteen years have gone by, but that's that's all you've been focused on.

So, no, you can't do anything about yesterday or tomorrow yet. You can make plans for the future, but all we've got to do is get through today.

Roy: Love the idea of mindfulness at Goodison!

When I stopped drinking in 2007, I was absolutely terrified of how I was going to navigate my way through life without my anesthetic. I was told to keep at it in the day. Don't worry about staying sober at hypothetical events that may or may not occur one month or twenty years in the future. I stayed sober yesterday and if I did similar things today, I could also stay sober today. I did it. It's turned into the best part of twenty years in recovery. I still use it now. Not in regard to drinking, just in regards to life and the obstacles I face. Doing my best not to flap about the future or worry about the past. It's all easier said than done but it still underpins my life now. Living life a day at a time doesn't mean you can't make plans or have ambitions. It just means you can't control the outcome of them. All we can do is do our bit as best we can.

When speaking to you, Neville, it was clear you weren't falling for the divide and tactics. Hence your Twitter takeovers by groups who want to support those seeking asylum, as well as people who can dispel some of the myths around transgenderism or those recovering from addiction, for example. My own workplace has taken over your account a few times. Only goodness has come from it. My day job is at Damien John Kelly House in Liverpool, a recovery living centre for adult males who are recovering from addiction. When you work with people who are making changes and facing hurdles seemingly at every corner, you tend to learn a lot about yourself. You identify with them. You believe in fairness, justice, balance and seeing the potential in your fellow human beings. You want to learn more.

Neville: Yes, exactly. What you've got to realise is that when you're a footballer, you live in bubble because you're so focused on the game. So after my career ended, Twitter opened my eyes. Once I popped that football bubble, my world opened up. A sportsperson's life is incredibly selfish; getting *yourself* ready to be the best you can be every day, and that's it.

Social media helped me understand the world around me better, and that what's key is education. It can be simple stuff, like talking to people who know about the things I don't. The reason I did the takeovers was to understand people better and help others do the same. I can't just do that myself, can I, because I don't have a fucking clue. So, I gave my Twitter to other people to explain their lives.

Roy: That's the one, Nev: listening to other people's experiences rather than remaining stuck and rigid, particularly on subjects we don't really know much about. Whatever form of recovery you're in, you never really stay still. You'll feel stuck, but it's usually just that the small changes made take a while for us to really feel the benefits. The way to keep moving in the right direction is to open your eyes, ears and heart to others. Just because we feel a particular way about something, or would deal with something in our own way, doesn't necessarily mean it's the right way. It's just the way we know and have become comfortable with. Get uncomfortable! While at the same time, learn to appreciate what's in front of you right now. Breathe. Deeply. A few times. It works.

Keeping it in the day. Twenty-four hours. With that in mind, we came up with the idea of writing our twenty-four suggestions. (We've blatantly stolen the loose idea from Bob Mortimer's rules for life.) Me and Neville aren't experts. Like Cold War Steve, we're just having a go. There will be no linked-in inspirational quotes, no 'grind' waffle about getting up at 3 a.m. and doing seven million sit ups before drinking twelve raw eggs and getting into the office at 5 a.m. I promise.

TWENTY-FOUR HOUR HEARTY PEOPLE

ROY & NEVILLE SOUTHALL

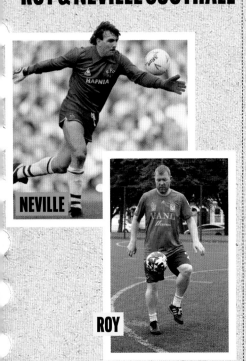

NEVILLE

ROY

1. If you can help, then help. Just make sure you're in a position to help. If you were on an aircraft that was in trouble and wanted to help others, you would have to put your own oxygen mask on first in order to help others. It's not about being selfish, ever. It's just about giving yourself and others the best possible chance.

2. Get some decent socks. There is no excuse for shit socks. You can get a half decent pair on the cheap these days.

3. Do something you wouldn't usually do: watch a subtitled film, listen to some classical music, try that food you are convinced you will not like, write down how you feel. Obviously, don't go too far . . . do not vote for *them*.

4. Make sure the people you love and care about know that you love and care about them. Tell them. However hard it might feel. Do it for them . . . but you'll feel good as a result as well.

5. Never pass up the chance to mentally rate any cock and balls graffiti you may notice on your travels. Consider the following: bollock size, hair, ejaculation detail. These things matter.

6. Never trust someone who says, 'Never trust someone who doesn't like football'.

7. Find your crew, wherever they are. They might be in a writing group, yoga class, recovery session, drumming tribe, LGBTQ community, a bunch of arl arses down the alehouse. Belonging is everything.

8. Have people in your life who love you enough to tell you when you're being a bit of a knobhead.

9. Tell the truth with compassion. Without compassion, it can be cruel. Those media 'straight talkers'? You know the type. Don't end up like that.

10. Try as many different cheeses as you can. When you find the ones you love, cherish them with all your heart. Cheese is life.

11. Live longer. Reduce your chances of having a heart attack: don't watch Question Time.

12. Pass it on. Whether it's a great song, a brilliant film, an inspiring speech, a beautiful painting, a tasty chippy, a method of reducing anxiety. Tell people about it. It's the complete opposite of materialism. When you share something material, it'll soon be gone.

13. Practice looking in the mirror and saying three very important words to yourself. You're going to need these words: I don't know. Don't be a know-it-all. Nobody like a smart arse.

14. It's never too late to have a happy childhood.

15. If the usual 'hate for cash' commentators are up in arms about a subject (whatever it may be on that particular week), remember that they're usually just distracting you from their own greed, lies and cruelty.

16. Stroke a dog at any given opportunity.

17. 'It's the hope that kills you.' No, it isn't. Hope keeps you alive. There is always hope.

18. We need people. Connection is vital. Make sure you've got some time for yourself too. A table for one in a café, a solo trip to the cinema, a peaceful sit down on a park bench with a butty. You can be good company for yourself.

19. Have faith. In whatever you like. We like to have it in Good.

20. Accepting something doesn't mean you agree with it. This regime – that's what it is – can tire us out. We're just preserving your energy for an area where we can affect change, in our own immediate worlds and communities.

21. We encourage rituals and structure. Whether it's getting up a bit earlier and sitting down for a brew in the morning, going for a walk in the evening or getting into that wildlife documentary, do what keeps you anchored. Watching Question Time doesn't count.

22. Write on the sole of your slipper with a biro. Try it. Cheers Nige.

23. Watch anything Bob Mortimer is in.

24. Stick with the winners. People who make you flourish. We all want to feel love, purpose, belonging and connection. We can do it in unison. Include people. Regardless of their race, gender, sexuality, whatever their pronouns. Don't forget to try those cheeses either. ●

PJ Smith is a writer from north Liverpool and is otherwise known as Roy. Neville Southall is the former Everton and Welsh international goalkeeping legend and political activist. They are both very good blokes.

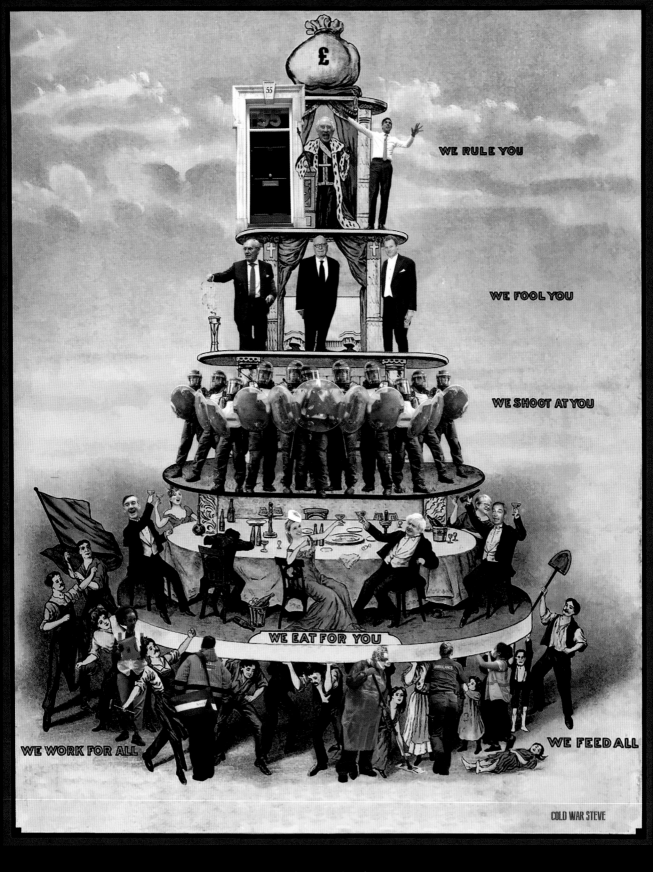

WE RULE YOU

WE FOOL YOU

WE SHOOT AT YOU

WE EAT FOR YOU

WE WORK FOR ALL

WE FEED ALL

COLD WAR STEVE

The Conservatives' thirteen years in power began with the sheer cruelty of austerity – a policy which impacted the poorest and most vulnerable in society. We are now in a cost-of-living crisis and people are having to choose between eating or heating. Thankfully Thérèse Coffey and other Cabinet members have been on hand with invaluable advice, such as 'eat more turnips' or 'just get a better paid job'.

THE CONSERVATIVE ANTI-GROWTH COALITION
12 YEARS IN POWER

Steve's FISH BAR

Just get a second job, or a better paid job

FOOD BANK

The Covid/lockdown period appeared to be enabling, at least initially, the scales to fall from the public's eyes. It became demonstrably clear that so-called 'low-skilled' workers were much more important to our way of life than multi-billionaire tax dodgers and venal right-wing commentators. NHS workers were applauded from doorsteps across the country. Now those very same workers, nurses and doctors are vilified for having the audacity of not wanting to be overworked (to breaking point) and undervalued.

PAN-PACIFIC MEAT, SHOES & FANCY GOODS

CPTPP

2 £10

9.99

7.99

CPTPP

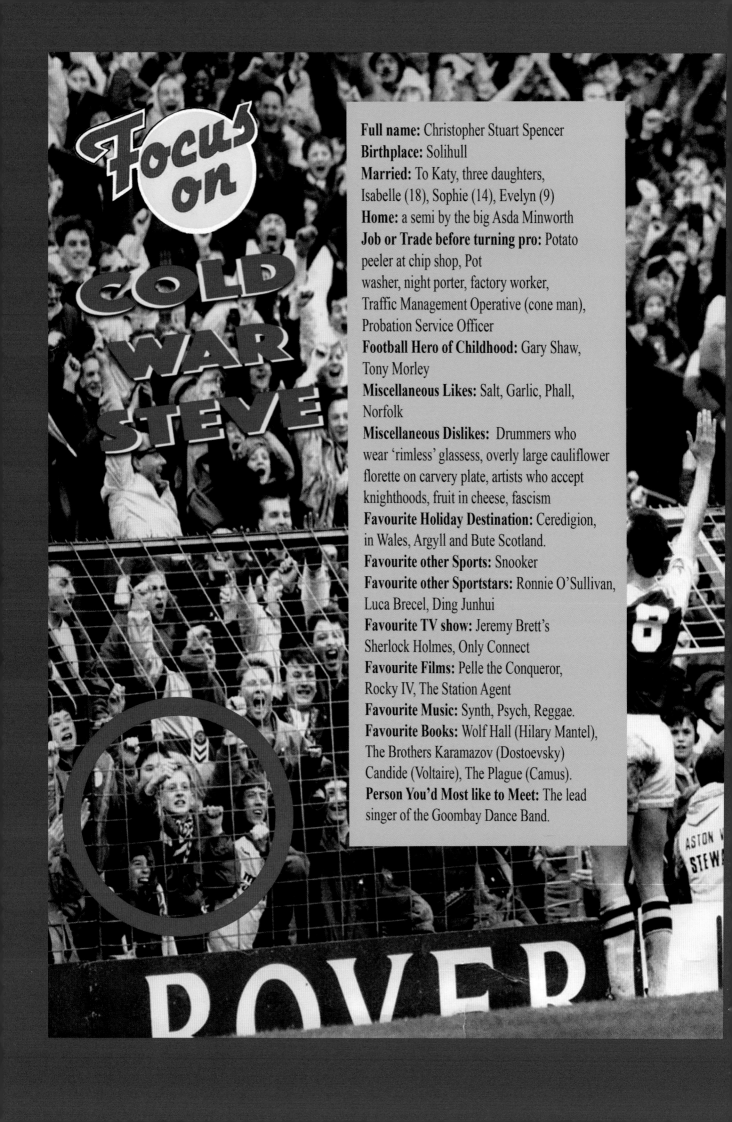

Focus on COLD WAR STEVE

Full name: Christopher Stuart Spencer
Birthplace: Solihull
Married: To Katy, three daughters, Isabelle (18), Sophie (14), Evelyn (9)
Home: a semi by the big Asda Minworth
Job or Trade before turning pro: Potato peeler at chip shop, Pot washer, night porter, factory worker, Traffic Management Operative (cone man), Probation Service Officer
Football Hero of Childhood: Gary Shaw, Tony Morley
Miscellaneous Likes: Salt, Garlic, Phall, Norfolk
Miscellaneous Dislikes: Drummers who wear 'rimless' glassess, overly large cauliflower florette on carvery plate, artists who accept knighthoods, fruit in cheese, fascism
Favourite Holiday Destination: Ceredigion, in Wales, Argyll and Bute Scotland.
Favourite other Sports: Snooker
Favourite other Sportstars: Ronnie O'Sullivan, Luca Brecel, Ding Junhui
Favourite TV show: Jeremy Brett's Sherlock Holmes, Only Connect
Favourite Films: Pelle the Conqueror, Rocky IV, The Station Agent
Favourite Music: Synth, Psych, Reggae.
Favourite Books: Wolf Hall (Hilary Mantel), The Brothers Karamazov (Dostoevsky) Candide (Voltaire), The Plague (Camus).
Person You'd Most like to Meet: The lead singer of the Goombay Dance Band.